D1518553

THAT ROCKS!

THE ROCK CYCLE

By Maria Nelson

Gareth Stevens
Publishing

Please visit our website, www.garethstevens.com. For a free color catalog of all our high-quality books, call toll free 1-800-542-2595 or fax 1-877-542-2596.

Library of Congress Cataloging-in-Publication Data

Nelson, Maria.
 The rock cycle / Maria Nelson.
     p. cm. — (That rocks!)
 Includes index.
 ISBN 978-1-4339-8326-9 (pbk.)
 ISBN 978-1-4339-8327-6 (6-pack)
  ISBN 978-1-4339-8325-2 (library binding)
 1. Rocks—Juvenile literature. 2. Fossils—Juvenile literature. I. Title.
 QE432.2.N43 2014
 552—dc23
                                      2012047235

First Edition

Published in 2014 by
Gareth Stevens Publishing
111 East 14th Street, Suite 349
New York, NY 10003

Copyright © 2014 Gareth Stevens Publishing

Designer: Katelyn Londino
Editor: Kristen Rajczak

Photo credits: Cover, p. 1 Claudio Rossol/Shutterstock.com; p. 5 Krishna.Wu/Shutterstock.com; p. 7 Lukiyanova Natalia/frenta/ Shutterstock.com; pp. 9, 17, 19 iStockphoto/Thinkstock.com; p. 11 Simon Krzic/Shutterstock.com; p. 13 Nik Azwaa Photography/ Flickr/Getty Images; p. 15 © iStockphoto.com/prill; p. 20 (inset) InStock Photographic Ltd./Photodisc/Getty Images.

Printed in the United States of America

CPSIA compliance information: Batch #CS13GS: For further information contact Gareth Stevens, New York, New York at 1-800-542-2595.

CONTENTS

A New Idea 4

Inside Earth 6

Introducing the Rock Types 8

Begin with Breakdown 10

On the Move 12

From Sediment to Rock 14

The Great Melt 16

On Top of the World 18

Rock Cycle Study 20

Glossary 22

For More Information 23

Index 24

Words in the glossary appear in **bold** type the first time they are used in the text.

A NEW IDEA

During the 1700s, scientists had many questions about the makeup and age of Earth. They studied rocks and **fossils** but couldn't explain what they found. Then, Scottish scientist John Hutton presented a new idea. He said that the rock that made up Earth had been slowly forming, breaking down, and reforming in the same way for a long time.

Today, Hutton's idea is used in a model called the rock cycle. A cycle is a series of steps that repeats over time.

SET IN STONE

Rock is the nonliving solid matter that makes up Earth. It forms naturally and can contain many different kinds of **minerals**.

From Waikiki Beach in Hawaii to the Rocky Mountains, different forms of rock can be found all over the world.

INSIDE EARTH

Since James Hutton wrote about **geology** in the 1700s, scientists have learned a lot about Earth. They discovered that the planet has three layers: a hard outer crust, a hot mantle, and an even hotter, liquid core.

Together, the crust and solid upper part of the mantle are called the lithosphere. It's divided into moveable slabs of rock called plates. The plates slide past one another, **collide**, and slip under and over each other. The lithosphere is where the rock cycle mainly happens.

SET IN STONE

Scientists who study the history and form of Earth are called geologists. They've used rocks to find that oceans once covered ancient Earth!

crust

upper mantle

lower mantle

core

The crust is what we think of as Earth because it's what we see.
However, it's a very small part of the planet.

INTRODUCING THE ROCK TYPES

Earth's crust is mainly made up of sedimentary rock. This rock forms from the pressing together of tiny bits of rock—such as sand, clay, or pebbles—called sediment. Metamorphic rock forms from existing rock that changes in order to remain **stable** under new conditions, such as increased temperature. Igneous rock forms from the cooling of hot, melted rock rising from within Earth.

All three kinds of rock have a part in the rock cycle. Read on to find out how this amazing Earth **process** begins!

SET IN STONE

Igneous processes are the only way for new rock to form.

The rock cycle shows how each kind of rock can become either of the other two. The shale of this rock face is sedimentary, but under the right conditions, it can become the metamorphic rock called slate.

BEGIN WITH BREAKDOWN

The rock cycle model starts with weathering, or the breakdown of rock into sediment. Weathering can happen when water flows into a rock and freezes, causing it to crack. Mixtures of water and minerals can cause **chemical** changes in rock, making it soft enough to fall apart. Wind blowing over rock for a long time can weather it, too.

Tiny living things called bacteria give off chemicals that break down rock. Animals also cause weathering by scratching or digging in rock.

SET IN STONE

Sediment may be made of the tiny shells of ocean animals. These collect on the ocean floor.

Weathering that occurs because of a living thing, such as an animal, is called biological weathering.

ON THE MOVE

Sediment created by weathering often moves. The wearing away of rock into sediment and its movement is called erosion. Wind and water are both common means of erosion. **Gravity** may also cause erosion. It pulls loose rock down mountains in rock slides. It causes mudflows down hills when rain softens certain kinds of rock.

After a time, sediment settles in a place. Over time, more sediment settles on top of it.

SET IN STONE

Erosion can be caused by **glaciers**. They melt and refreeze in cracks of rock. They also push rock apart as they slowly move, sometimes carrying the rock and causing it to grind against other rock.

While important to the rock cycle,
erosion like rock slides can crush cars and homes.

FROM SEDIMENT TO ROCK

As more matter buries sediment, the **pressure** on it increases and causes it to **compact**. Water mixtures flow into open spaces in the rock, leaving behind minerals that bind the sediment together. This is sedimentary rock!

Some rock stays in this form. Some continues to be forced deeper in Earth and becomes metamorphic rock. As the conditions around the rock change—such as an increase in temperature and pressure—its chemical makeup changes.

SET IN STONE

The movement of Earth's plates is one way rock can be pushed below Earth's surface. This movement can also cause rocks to fold and break.

The bits of rock and other matter that make up sedimentary rock are called clasts. Clasts can be tiny—like a grain of sand—or as large as a pebble!

THE GREAT MELT

Both increased temperature and changes in the pressure on a rock can cause rock to melt. This liquid rock is called magma when it's under Earth's surface. Igneous rock forms when magma rises and cools in pockets and tunnels underground.

Increased pressure forces magma out of cracks in Earth's surface or the weak places where plates meet. Magma is called lava when it's above the ground. The places lava bursts from are volcanoes! Igneous rocks form from this cooled lava, too.

SET IN STONE

Igneous rock can build up around the site of an active volcano, forming the mountain shape of many famous volcanoes.

Rocks melt at different temperatures and pressures depending on what minerals they're made up of.

ON TOP OF THE WORLD

Just as the movement of Earth's plates can cause rock to be forced deeper underground, plates colliding may raise rock to the surface. This is called uplift—and it's one of the most important parts of the rock cycle.

Uplift pushes rock that forms underground to Earth's surface as mountains and hills. The rock then faces weathering to begin the rock cycle again. Without uplift, the rock cycle would stop after a time. Existing rock, mountains, and hills would wear away completely.

SET IN STONE

The movement of Earth's plates may also cause the ground to shake in an earthquake!

Earth's plates are always moving. However, they move very slowly.

ROCK CYCLE STUDY

The rock cycle is an ongoing process with no real beginning or end. It's been going on since Earth formed—and it's going on right now!

Since James Hutton's time, scientists have studied not only the rock cycle, but also how long it takes. They can figure out how old a rock is and figure out what kind of rock it is by looking at its chemical makeup. This has helped them learn that our planet is about 4.6 billion years old. That's some ancient rock!

THE ROCK CYCLE

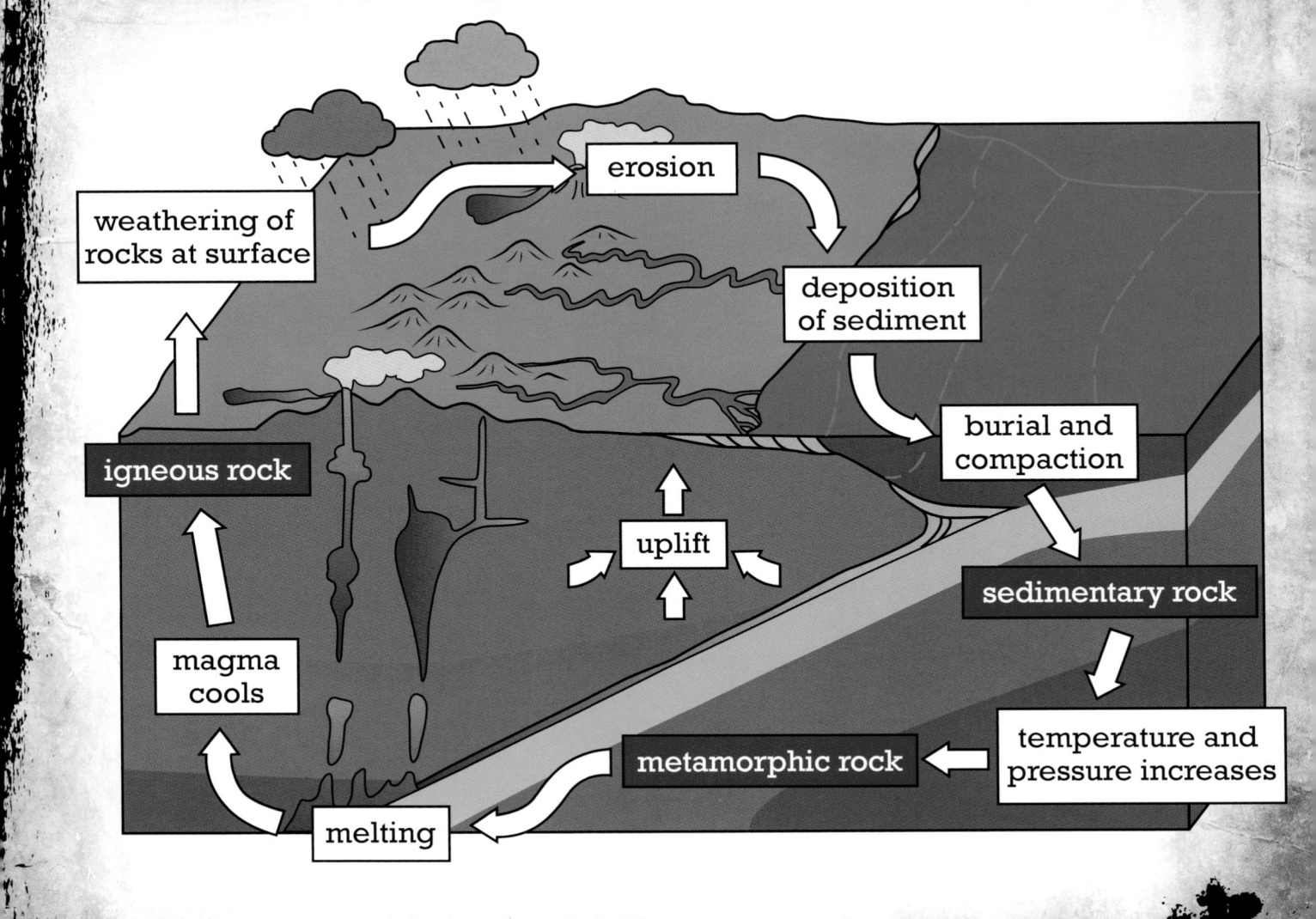

GLOSSARY

chemical: having to do with matter that can be mixed with other matter to cause changes. Also, the matter itself.

collide: the hitting of two objects against one another

compact: forcing things closer together

fossil: the marks or remains of plants and animals that lived long ago

geology: the science that studies the history of Earth and its life as recorded in rocks

glacier: a large body of ice that moves slowly

gravity: the force that pulls objects toward Earth's center

mineral: matter in the ground that forms rocks

pressure: the application of force

process: the set of steps that move something forward

stable: not likely to change suddenly or greatly

FOR MORE INFORMATION

Books

Bryan, Bethany. *How the Rock Cycle Works*. New York, NY: PowerKids Press, 2009.

Morgan, Sally. *Rocks*. Mankato, MN: Smart Apple Media, 2012.

Websites

How Rocks & Minerals Are Formed
www.rocksforkids.com/RFK/howrocks.html
Read more about the different kinds of rocks, what they're made of, and how they form.

Rocky's Journey Around the Rock Cycle
www.oum.ox.ac.uk/thezone/rocks/cycle/index.htm
Use an interactive graphic of the rock cycle to learn more about this process.

INDEX

chemicals 10, 14, 20

clasts 15

core 6, 7

crust 6, 7, 8

erosion 12, 13, 21

fossils 4

glaciers 12

gravity 12

Hutton, John 4, 6, 20

igneous rock 8, 16, 21

lava 16

lithosphere 6

magma 16, 21

mantle 6, 7

metamorphic rock 8, 9, 14, 21

minerals 4, 10, 14, 17

plates 6, 14, 16, 18, 19

pressure 14, 16, 17, 21

sedimentary rock 8, 9, 14, 15

temperature 14, 16, 17, 21

uplift 18, 21

volcanoes 16

water 10, 12, 14

weathering 10, 11, 12, 18, 21

wind 10, 12